D1432954

RANDOLPH CALDECOTT

Engraved from Randolph Caldecott's last photograph.
From the Brasenose Club Catalogue.

RANDOLPH CALDECOTT

1846-1886

An Appreciation

By MARY GOULD DAVIS

J. B. Lippincott Company
PHILADELPHIA & NEW YORK

The illustrations are reproduced from early prints of Caldecott drawings through the courtesy of The Houghton Memorial Library of Harvard University, The New York Public Library, and Mr. Frederic Melcher.

The jacket illustration, long familiar as the cover design of *The Horn Book*, is made available through the courtesy of the Magazine.

PART ONE

The Picture Books

From *The Three Jovial Huntsmen*

From *The Farmer's Boy*

WHEN the children look at Randolph Caldecott's picture books they turn the pages very slowly. Each page tells a story, first in the action, then in the characters and, finally, in the little details that children love to linger over. Their eyes turn occasionally to the words on the opposite page, but only for a moment. Then they go back to the pictures. Often the poem or the nursery rhyme that is illustrated is known to them; but Randolph Caldecott's interpretation of that rhyme is a new and delightful adventure. Their eyes follow John Gilpin in his mad gallop over the countryside and through the narrow streets of an English village; they scan the wintry fields for the tiny distant figures of the Three Jovial Huntsmen; they linger soberly on the bedroom scene, in *The Babes in the Woods*, where the old Nurse brings the Babes to say good-bye to their dying parents. Little boys sometimes look slightly sheepish as they follow the romantic history of *A Frog He Would A-Wooing Go*, but little girls smile and glance at one another with that look that is purely feminine—and as old as Eve.

Caldecott's creative imagination is never more in evidence than in the story of the lovelorn frog. He is so gallant, so appealing in his green coat

7

and pale blue waistcoat, with his hat under his arm and a bouquet of flowers for his ladylove in one hand. He is carrying a cane, too, and the people who are fishing in the river stare at him in admiration as he goes by. When he meets Mr. Rat and they start off together they are tiny figures in the background while, in the foreground, a mother and her two little girls sit under a tree and watch them.

It is when they come to Miss Mousie's house that the excitement really begins. How charming and demure she is in her white muslin dress with a wide ruffle around her neck and a pink sash tied around her slender waist! She serves them beer in tall glasses from a flagon that might be a family heirloom. Mr. Frog drinks freely, but his wooing is always uppermost in his mind. Little girls linger for a long time over the drawing where he is kissing Miss Mousie's tail, while Mr. Rat sits in a chair against the wall with his legs crossed and the glass of beer in his hand. Mr. Rat does not look jealous; he looks bold and comfortable and perhaps a bit sleepy. Children from the Southern States often think that Mr. Rat is not another suitor, but Miss Mousie's uncle. This is because in the South there is a longer version of the story, that tells many more details than the original English version. It is very long indeed—verse after verse, like the cowboy ballads—and it gives many details of the wedding that never occurred:

> "O Uncle Rat he went to town,
>   Um, um-m-m-m-
> O Uncle Rat he went to town
> To buy his niece a weddin' gown.
>   Um, um-m-m-m-."

The drawing of "a cat and her kittens came tumbling in" is an original interpretation. It is good to hear the children chuckle over it. Here is Miss Mousie's cottage surrounded by trees, in green leaf, and a garden. A father, a mother and two children are standing in the path watching with interest

From *A Frog He Would A-Wooing Go*

while Mrs. Pussy, dressed in flowered muslin, creeps cautiously up the steps, followed by three kittens, also dressed in flowered muslin, their full skirts draped neatly over their tails. They look very respectable! Nevertheless, they get Mr. Rat and Miss Mousie, while Mr. Frog jumps out of the window—only to meet his tragic end when "a lily-white duck comes and gobbles him up."

It pleases the children that Caldecott made the King and Queen so youthful in *Sing a Song for Sixpence*. The interior of the counting house where the boy King is counting out his money repays long study. On the outside a footman has his ear pressed against the door while two agitated gentlemen, a Grenadier Guard, and another footman watch him anxiously. Inside, in the pleasant room, there is a clock, a calendar and a statue of St. George and the Dragon on the mantelpiece; and on the wall hang two very interesting paintings: one of Jack defying a truly terrible giant, and one of Robinson Crusoe and his man Friday. The crown is laid carefully on a velvet cushion on the table within reach of the King's hand. The Queen's parlor is even more repaying. The paintings on the wall there are

of Red Riding Hood, The Babes in the Woods, and Bo-Peep. There is a very regal-looking doll sitting on a chair beside the Queen; and in a cupboard near by is a group of puppets—Italian, by the look of them. You may be very sure that the children miss none of this! How tempting the honey looks with the loaf of crusty bread beside it. And how good the jars of jam look in *The Queen of Hearts*. The children count them over: apricot, black currant, peach, strawberry, raspberry, green gage, and three more jars that one cannot quite make out. In the Parker Collection at Harvard there is a de luxe edition of *The Queen of Hearts*. It is bound in red morocco, beautifully tooled, and there is a playing card of the Queen of Hearts set in the leather cover.

Younger boys and girls have a great affection for Baby Bunting. That little round face beneath the famous "rabbit skin" when the baby stands on a chair, with the rabbit ears sticking up cockily and the "rear" of the skin

dragging behind him, is irresistible. A nice touch is the drawing of the family dog, a spaniel, ears and tail up, following the baby's father when he starts off to shoot the rabbit. All that can be seen of father is the back of one foot disappearing around a corner of the wall; but you know exactly how the dog will feel if he is left behind.

Although one feels that Caldecott cared more for dogs than for cats, he has drawn some very effective members of the cat family. There is the family in *A Frog He Would A-Wooing Go*, there is the angry cat in *The House that Jack Built* and, best of all, there is the cat in *Hey Diddle Diddle* who played the fiddle so well. We see him first with the fiddle in his hands bowing graciously to four adorable children who are evidently lost in admiration of his powers. In another scene—the one when everyone begins to dance—the cow and the two pigs with rows of buttons up and down their fronts are just "stepping out" while the cat, dressed in a bright red coat, sits on a brick wall and fiddles vigorously. Even the two roosters are dancing, but "the little dog" sits quietly beside the wall and smiles. It is only later that he "laughs to see the sport." Over the two "dish ran away with the spoon" drawings the children spend a long time. How demure the Spoon looks as she sits on the bench with the Dish beside her. The cat is sitting on the dresser, still fiddling, and even the plates on the shelf above him have developed legs and are just about to jump down and join in the dance. Once a little girl who had just heard the story of *The Wedding of the Rag Doll and the Broom Handle* by Carl Sandburg found this picture and brought it, with dancing eyes, to the storyteller. "They are eloping, too," she said. So a great American poet and a great English artist bring life and drama to inanimate things, just as Hans Andersen did before them. It is often the little boys who discover in *The Milkmaid* that the snobbish-looking grayhound who comes with the "Sir" is approaching the farm collie with the same question that his master is asking "the pretty maid." Obviously, he gets very much the same answer. In the last drawing the collie is chasing the grayhound out of the field as enthusiastically as the milkmaids are chasing the fine gentleman.

As one grows older the picture books that linger longest in memory are perhaps *The Three Jovial Huntsmen* and *The Fox Jumped Over the Parson's Gate*. Here is the very heart of England; the roads, the wintry fields, the graceful bared branches of the trees. As we follow the huntsmen the melody of

"Do ye ken John Peel?"

keeps time to their galloping feet. Is it the Parson's mother who sits flat on the ground with a horrified expression while the hounds stream through the garden? Although the hounds will stop for nothing, we must pause a moment to study the gravestones in the churchyard. Says one: "Underneath lie the remains of Peter Piper who Picked a Peck . . ." The next one is "erected to the memory of Timothy Blowhorn." You cannot quite read the inscription on the others in the drawing where Nancy is coming out of the church on the arm of her soldier, but how lovely Nancy is in her poke bonnet wreathed with daisies and her white dress and yellow sash. Two earlier drawings of Caldecott's foretold the three huntsmen. They appeared in *The London Graphic* and are called "Hunting in the Midlands," "Going to Cover," and "Full Cry." Edmund Evans, the engraver, says that he does not know where Caldecott got the verses, but he *does* know that the verse about the Alderman was written by the artist himself.

Perhaps Caldecott's most original interpretation is of Mrs. Mary Blaize in Dr. Goldsmith's poem. This picture book does not mean so much to the little children as it does to the older boys and girls who are able to appreciate its gentle satire. In "she freely lent to all the poor who left a pledge behind," Caldecott makes Mrs. Blaize a pawnbroker. She stands behind the counter in a very interesting shop holding a young gallant's watch, while

From *The Great Panjandrum Himself*

with the other hand she pushes two coins toward him. In the next drawing a less attractive gentleman is leaving his waistcoat on the counter while he hastily buttons his coat over the place left vacant. How cold, how hard her face is as she turns away from the man who is trying to get even a small sum for his golden heart. In this drawing the little "R.C." that appears on every one is traced on the tablet hanging from the counter. Doubtless, Mrs. Blaize kept it there to record her dubious transactions. We feel not too much regret as we come to the final picture of Mrs. Blaize being carried into the churchyard in her coffin.

Why did Caldecott make the Great Panjandrum Himself a college professor in cap and gown with a Latin Grammar under one arm and a very realistic bundle of switches in his hand? He completely loses his dignity— to the joy of the children—in the game of catch-as-catch-can, and after it is over he looks so utterly exhausted that we can only feel sorry for him. The Great She-bear in this book is an unfailing favorite. She walks sedately along the village street with its lovely vistas, her dress of muslin dotted with red roses, with her neat red shoes and a red sash. She is carrying a basket for her marketing and an umbrella. The people who turn to look at her are amused and interested—and not at all frightened.

The children's faces are very sober as they turn the pages of *The Babes in the Woods*. Three generations have grieved over their sad fate. How many grandfathers and grandmothers there must be today who remember vividly those two adorable children and the wicked uncle with his pointed red beard and his black velvet doublet and hose.

After Caldecott's death in 1886, Frederick Warne issued a facsimile of the original sketches in ink for *The House that Jack Built*. And in the Parker Collection is the notebook, of the same size as the picture books, in which he made, in pencil, the first sketches for *The Babes in the Woods*. Most of his notebooks are the "pocket" kind, long and narrow, bound in

Till Robin-redbreast painfully
Did cover them with leaves.

From *The Babes in the Woods*

black cloth. There are twelve of them in the Parker Collection, and one can spend hours, even days, going over them. It is fascinating to trace the evolution of the scenes and the characters in the picture books. Here are the five mournful hounds who grieve over the death of the Mad Dog. It is a source of great satisfaction to the children that, in the finished design, Caldecott added the impressive black-edged card inscribed "In Memory of Toby." In the notebooks, too, are the hens and roosters that appear in *The Farmer's Boy,* and the swans. There are also many studies of pigs.

Pages are filled with the details of pigs: snouts, little eyes, tails, backs, legs. It is interesting to note the difference between Caldecott's pigs and the pigs of Leslie Brooke, who so worthily upheld the Caldecott tradition in English picture books. Leslie Brooke drew many of his pigs as reputable citizens of an orderly world, living in neat well-furnished cottages with portraits of their porcine ancestors hanging on the walls. Caldecott's pigs are more realistic. See them at the trough, waiting to be fed, in *The Farmer's Boy.* See the one wallowing happily in the mud in *The House that Jack Built.* True, the pigs who are dancing in *Hey Diddle Diddle* have rows of elegant buttons up and down their fronts. And, in *The Farmer's Boy,* there is an elderly pig in spectacles who is laboriously spelling out the word "Mary" with blocks. In *The Three Jovial Huntsmen* the pig is fat and jolly. There is some discussion about him:

> "One said it was a fat pig, but another he said 'Nay,
> It's just a Lunnon Alderman whose clothes were stole away.'"

Perhaps the most convincing pig of all is indicated in an early notebook and found in its final form in Hallam Tennyson's rhymed version of *Jack and the Beanstalk,* published by Macmillan in the year of Caldecott's death.

The studies of birds in the notebooks are especially interesting. Every possible detail is drawn, with marginal notes indicating corrections to be made for the final drawings. The notebooks are not always dated, so one does not know how many of these penciled sketches formed the basis for the hens and roosters, the ducks and swans in the picture books. Some were probably used for the illustrations in Mrs. Frederick Locker's *What the Blackbird Said*. Possibly Caldecott used them in his oil paintings of storks and pelicans for decorative screens.

It was Edmund Evans who suggested the plan for the picture books, in 1876. Evans' fame as an engraver is almost as great as Caldecott's fame as an artist. He engraved on wood the drawings of Walter Crane and Kate Greenaway as well as Caldecott's. What an exciting place his "enlarged establishment" at 116 Fleet Street must have been. He began his work when he was little more than a boy, working as an apprentice with Ebenezer Landells, first on Fleet Street and then at Landells' home at Barnsbury near Islington. In 1847 he set up his own establishment, and twenty years later was making the engravings for Walter Crane's *A Gaping, Wide-Mouthed Waddling Frog*. Many of the sketches for *London Society* and *The London Graphic* by various contemporary artists were engraved by Evans. He was deeply impressed with Caldecott's illustrations for the selections from Washington Irving's *Sketch Book*, engraved on wood by James Cooper. "I thought Randolph Caldecott," he says, "would be just the man to do some shilling toy books which I was anxious to do, so I appointed a meeting with him at his lodgings in Great Russell Street." Caldecott liked the idea and they began the work immediately. They decided upon blocks for six colors; dark brown, flesh tint, red, blue, yellow, and gray. It is characteristic of him that Caldecott refused an outright payment for his work, preferring to "share in the speculation." The first two printed were *John Gilpin* and *The House that Jack Built*. They were published by the house of George Routledge & Sons. Evans speaks of the first sketches that "were little more than outlines, but they were so racy and spontaneous." One can see these

first sketches now in the Parker Collection and in the facsimile of *The House that Jack Built,* published later by Frederick Warne. As to Caldecott's models, Evans says, "R. C. generally drew from his friends where a man was wanted; his cats, dogs, cows show how thoroughly he understood the anatomy of them." The drawings were made in pen and ink on a smooth-faced writing paper, photographed on wood and engraved "in facsimile." Only the lucky booklovers of today who own an early edition know how rich and glowing the colors were.

John Gilpin and *The House that Jack Built* sold for one shilling each and were an immediate success. The first ten thousand copies were sold well before a second printing could be made. Between 1878 and 1885 sixteen picture books were issued through this happy partnership, first as single books, then bound in volumes with board covers, usually four to a volume as they are today. In several cases Caldecott made an extra drawing for the cover. An "edition de luxe" on larger paper, each copy numbered and signed by publisher and printer, sold immediately one thousand copies. "I wished," Evans says rather wistfully, "I had printed three or four thousand instead of one thousand." After Caldecott's death George Routledge published: *The Complete Collection of Pictures and Songs by Randolph Caldecott.* (Engraved and Printed by Edmund Evans. With a Preface by Austin Dobson.) There is a copy of it in the Children's Room of The New York Public Library.

It was in 1883 that Edmund Evans engraved and printed, and George Routledge published, *A Sketch-Book of R. Caldecott's.* It is now a rare book and a "collector's item," but the children would gladly accept it as a picture book if it could be re-issued. On the back of the title page is a facsimile of a sentence in Caldecott's writing: "Dedicated to everybody—but copyright reserved." On the opposite page is a drawing that would delight the children. We see, in full color, an umbrella dressed up in Kate Greenaway clothes leaning against a chair, while a group of reporters and artists rush frantically toward it with pencils and notebooks. Underneath it Caldecott has written: "Intense & searching students of Nature!" The subject of the *Sketch-Book* is the four seasons: spring, summer, autumn and winter. The tender greens and pale pinks of spring and the rich golden tints of the autumn scenes are particularly lovely. In the spring section there is an exquisite sketch of the old walls surrounding Siena in Italy, with the olive trees bending in a spring wind and a man with two oxen plowing the ground. On the next page there is a drawing of San Gimignano—that ancient city of square towers that was partially destroyed in the second World War. Here, too, is one of the most appealing of Caldecott's donkeys. Edmund Evans says, "The *Sketch-Book* was not a success—why, I could never understand." Perhaps it was because it fell between two groups of readers. The satire in it, gentle as it is, would be beyond the comprehension of the children. But

Intense & searching students of Nature

From *A Sketch-Book*

how many boys and girls would worry about that? The drawings in their humor and their beauty of design are timeless and ageless.

The Caroline Miller Parker Collection at The Houghton Memorial Library at Harvard has many of the original drawings for the picture books, as well as the pocket notebooks, many first editions and a collection of personal letters. In The New York Public Library is one page of the original drawings for *John Gilpin*. In their publication, year after year, the picture books have had unbroken continuity. Soon after Caldecott's death the firm of George Routledge & Sons became Routledge, Warne and Routledge. Later it became Frederick Warne & Company, the present publisher. Today, after two world wars and the bombing of London, all four of the volumes bound in boards and fourteen out of the sixteen single volumes are available. The enchanting little "miniature" edition is out of print. The Parker

Collection has the full set in single volumes and one copy of the four bound in boards.

On Randolph Caldecott's birthday, March 22nd, the picture books are taken from the shelves and the locked cases in the Children's Rooms of public libraries all over the country and placed within easy reach of the children's hands. His birthday and Kate Greenaway's—they were born in the same year—come within a few days of one another. They fall in "the spring of the year" and the children have learned to associate their books with yellow primroses and golden daffodils, with pussy willows and the young green of budding trees. Best of all, they have learned to think of England as Caldecott drew it—the England that can never die. Not the thing that man's hands have fashioned and that can be destroyed, but the very land itself: the fields that are green again with every spring, the little hills of Shropshire softly rounded against the sky, the walled gardens and quiet churchyards. Even the most exacting expert can find no fault with Caldecott's drawing of the domestic animals, while his humor, his tolerance, his integrity as an artist bring his people to life on every page—all sorts and kinds of people from the members of Parliament to the kindly, weather-beaten old farmers at the cattle fairs.

That contemporary artists appreciated Caldecott's work is shown by the tributes paid him at the memorial exhibition of his pictures in Manchester in 1888. It was held at the Brasenose Club; and the official catalogue in the Parker Collection quotes the speeches from famous people of the day. Vincent van Gogh valued his sketches highly. In a letter to Anton Ridder van Rappard in 1883 he speaks of collecting the sketches published in English magazines: "Caldecott does such splendid work," he says. There is a nice tribute to him from a contemporary (now known only as A.T-B), in the preface to the facsimile edition of the first sketches for *John Gilpin*. "For Randolph Caldecott was a creator," he says, "a maker of types, and we have waited for him long. Once and for all he has shown us John Gilpin, once and for all the Man that the Mad Dog Bit and the Mad Dog itself, and the Three Jolly Huntsmen and many an old friend more."

In the *Routledge Magazine*, Christmas Number for 1881, there are three drawings in full, rich color: "Little Fanny," by Kate Greenaway, "Ride a Cockhorse" by Randolph Caldecott, and "Little Pandora" by Walter Crane —three English artists who have survived war and its aftermath and social changes; pictures whose value grows and deepens as a confused world seeks security and happiness for its children.

As long as books exist and there are children to enjoy them, boys and girls—and their elders—will turn the pages of the Caldecott picture books. They will follow John Gilpin's wild ride through pages that glow with vitality and color. They will feel the cold of the wintry English fields with the Three Jovial Huntsmen. They will grieve with the robins who covered the tiny bodies of the Babes in the Woods with autumn leaves, and laugh with the pigs who danced to the cat's fiddle. They will sit with the little Queen in her parlor "eating bread and honey" and walk with the lady-bear along the streets of an English village. New artists, new trends, new techniques will come and be welcomed. But Randolph Caldecott and his engraver, Edmund Evans, will remain unchallenged in their field.

From *A Frog He Would A-Wooing Go*

PART TWO

The Artist

From *Old Christmas*

From *The Fox Jumped Over the Parson's Gate*

RANDOLPH CALDECOTT was born in the old city of Chester in western England on the River Dee, where lived the famous Miller of the song, on March 22nd, 1846. Victoria had been Queen for nine years and married to the Prince Consort for seven of them. The Corn Laws had been repealed, and free trade was established in the year of his birth. There is no very clear record of his childhood. We know that he loved all birds and beasts, that he drew them, painted them, cut them out of wood and modeled them in clay. Perhaps those clumsy, childish fingers made the first model of the lovely bas-relief of later years called "Feeding the Calves." The boy loved to be out-of-doors in all weathers and at all times of the day; but as a pupil at the Henry VIII School in Chester he made a fine record.

When he was fifteen he left Chester and went to Whitchurch in Shropshire to work in a bank and live "in an old farmhouse about two miles from town where he used to go fishing and shooting, to the meets of hounds, to markets and cattle fairs." Perhaps it was then that he began to fill his notebooks with the sketches that later became his picture books. We know that

25

he often returned to Shropshire. In the spring of 1878, when he was twenty-nine years old and his reputation as an artist established, he wrote from Dodington near Whitchurch to a friend in London: "I feel that I owe somebody an apology for staying in the country for so long, but don't quite see to whom it is due, so I shall stay two or three days longer, and then I shall hang my harp on a willow tree. It is difficult to screw up the proper amount of courage to leave the lambkins, the piglets, the foals, the goslings, the calves and puppies." His love for animals and understanding of them, as well as his unfailing interest in people, is inherent in his work all through his life.

He was twenty when he went to Manchester to work there in the Manchester and Salford Bank. It was the first great change for him and he must have missed the country ways. But in Manchester he found kindred spirits and made lifelong friends. His life as an artist really began there. He joined the Brasenose Club and studied in the Manchester School of Art. He began to make sketches that appeared in local newspapers and magazines. Most of them were amusing drawings of contemporary people and events. An early one called "The First Quadrille" under the general heading "Manchester Society" is interesting when it is compared with the later ones that were published in *The London Graphic* and *London Society*. It shows how Caldecott's work strengthened during those years. It was Henry Blackburn, the editor of *London Society*, who four years after Caldecott's death brought these sketches together under the title *Randolph Caldecott's Sketches*. They were published by Sampson Low, in October, 1889. Some of them are carefully finished and beautiful in design, like the one of the pelicans called "A Morning Walk." Many are satirical—but not unkind. Years later A.T-B. was to say of him in the foreword of the facsimile edition of the original drawings for *The House that Jack Built:* "If he satirized human foibles he never satirized human faults; with all his knowledge of

The Artist

human character, he was a humorist who was never unkind." One of his
personal friends describing him in the Manchester years said: "The hand-
some lad carried his own recommendation. With light-brown hair falling
with a ripple over his brow, blue-gray eyes shaded with long lashes, sweet
and mobile mouth, tall and well-made—he joined to these physical advan-
tages a gay good humor and a charming disposition." In 1872 he gave up
his work for the bank and went to London to devote himself to his career as
an artist. It was an important decision. By this time he had good friends who
encouraged and helped him. Among them were Henry Blackburn, E. J.
Poynter under whom Caldecott studied, and the art director of the South
Kensington Museum, Mr. Armstrong, who gave him excellent advice.

He was twenty-six when he had his first glimpse of the Continent. With
Henry Blackburn he spent a summer exploring the Harz Mountains in
Germany. He brought back some sketches which were published first in
The London Graphic and later in a book for which Blackburn wrote the
text. It was called *The Harz Mountains; A Tour in the Toy Country* and
was published by Sampson Low in 1872. These sketches were also Caldecott's introduction to his public in America. Henry Blackburn took some of
them to the United States and they were published in *Harper's Monthly
Magazine* for 1873. One of the drawings, at least, foreshadows the picture
books. It is of a square in a mountain village and it has a Noah's-Ark-like quality. The trees and animals are set up in neat rows, while a very stiff gentleman
in a long buttoned coat talks to a peasant in the foreground. But the lion
and the ox among the animals have come to life and are saying things to
one another that one longs to hear! Although one of the sketches, the one
called "Our Guide at Gosler," is a perfect illustration of the "master race"
that started two world wars, Caldecott seems to have liked the Germans.
During a later trip to Germany he writes to a friend in London, "I like
German officers. I have found them polite and accomplished men, Aus-

27

trians being the most graceful in figure and manner." He then sketches on the letter a drawing of himself with a long cigar in one hand and a stein of beer in the other, a Prussian officer standing at his left and an Austrian officer on his right. He never seemed to have any trouble in getting people to serve as models on these Continental tours. Blackburn says that "the interviews were conducted slowly and gravely, ending in peals of laughter from the natives."

On his return from Germany, Caldecott settled down in London, painting, modeling and making drawings for an occasional book and for magazines and newspapers. For one daily newspaper he made a series of sketches of the old Law Courts at Westminster that have great value today. Under a very amusing sketch of the Solicitor General he wrote: "Cross examination of the plaintiff's principal witness by the Solicitor General (who wears a very untidy wig, by the way)." In 1873 he made the well-known sketch of John Bull, an Irishman and a Scotsman standing on the cliffs of southern England with a telescope, watching for the balloon from America that never came. "Excitement of the inhabitants of Great Britain on receipt of a telegram that it was actually on its way," it is captioned. Under one contemporary drawing of a lady in a very fashionable dress who is lifting her ruffled petticoats to show the tip of a dainty foot he writes: "Too short!" One entire notebook, now in the Parker Collection, is filled with sketches of people in London. They are all types, from flower-women and cabbies to members of Parliament.

During the summers of those first years in London he lived in a cottage that Henry Blackburn lent him at Farnham Royal near Windsor, using for his studio "a loose box adjoining a stable." It was here that he began to work on the illustrations for selections from Washington Irving's *Sketch Book*. Caldecott was always particularly fortunate in his engravers. James Cooper engraved the drawings for *Old Christmas* and *Bracebridge Hall*—those

From *Randolph Caldecott's Sketches*

two books that are such a happy combination of Irving's feeling for England and Caldecott's skill in interpreting it. With the generosity that is shown in all his personal contacts Caldecott gives Cooper equal credit for their success. In the dedication of the first edition he speaks of himself as the artist and Cooper as the engraver, saying—"Throughout they have worked together 'con amore.' With what success the public must decide." The public lost no time in making its decision. The two books won instant popularity and they established Caldecott's reputation as an illustrator. It is interesting to know that before Macmillan published *Old Christmas* in 1876 it had been offered to and refused by several publishers. One of them considered it "inartistic, flippant, vulgar and unworthy of the author of *Old Christmas*." If Washington Irving was listening to this comment from his place in Heaven he must have been amused.

During 1874 and 1875 Caldecott worked on the illustrations for a new edition of *Aesop's Fables*, with James Cooper again as the engraver. It was not published until the spring of 1883 and, for some reason, was not the success that both artist and engraver hoped that it would be. They called it: *Some of Aesop's Fables with Modern Instances*. (Shown in Designs by Randolph Caldecott. From New Translations by Alfred Caldecott. Engravings by James Cooper. Macmillan. London. 1883.) Caldecott yielded to Cooper in adding the "modern instances"—sketches of contemporary people and incidents on the page opposite each illustration for the *Fables*. It probably would have been wiser to omit them. They have little appeal to children and they are definitely dated. Otherwise, boys and girls would like the drawings for the *Fables*. Among them are some of Caldecott's most expressive dogs.

In the summer of 1874 Caldecott made his first journey to Brittany and liked it so much that he went again in 1878, traveling both times with Henry Blackburn. The two of them seem to have had a good many amusing adventures. The book, *Breton Folk; An Artistic Tour in Brittany*, with text by Blackburn and illustrations by Caldecott, was published by Sampson Low in 1880. The notebooks in the Parker Collection show a number of the Brittany sketches. Some of them were published first in *The London Graphic* and several appear in *Randolph Caldecott's Sketches*. There are three sketches in this volume, Blackburn tells us, which present the figure of the artist himself. In the first, called "Hard Work," he is leaning against the wall in a ballroom watching the gentlemen steer their ladies around the crowded floor. The second is a charming sketch of Caldecott sitting on the curb in front of an iron fence. A group of admiring children stand around him and a nurse holding a baby is watching his hands. The third scene is a game room in Monte Carlo. Caldecott has his back toward us as he watches the play at one of the tables. In the second sketch and, even more, in all of his photographs one wishes that the conventions of his day had not dictated that he wear a beard! That "mobile mouth" is always hidden. Only the brow and eyes are clear.

It was at about this time that he turned again to modeling, taking lessons from the French sculptor, Monsieur Balou, in London. He modeled some small figures of French peasants and two large bas-reliefs—"The Horse Fair in Brittany," finished and exhibited at The Royal Academy in 1878, and "The Boar Hunt," in 1879. His oil painting, "The Three Huntsmen," was a Royal Academy exhibit, too, in 1878. It is interesting to know that "The Three Huntsmen" was bought by a Mr. Mundella whose small granddaughter served as a model for the little Queen in *Sing a Song for Sixpence*. An amusing sidelight on Caldecott's feeling about being lionized appears in a letter to Mrs. Mundella, who had evidently asked him to come to tea. "I shall be happy to have tea with you," he writes "even if there *will* be authoresses present." His oil painting of "The Three Ravens" is now in the Parker Collection, and there, too, is the bas-relief in wax called "Feeding the Calves" and two in bronze—"The Jovial Huntsmen" and "The Diligence."

His trip to Italy in 1877 was partly a retreat from the cold and dampness of England and a search for the sun. His health, never very good, had begun to fail although one would never have guessed it from his letters, which are a better index to his personality than anything that has been written about him. Many of them are in the Parker Collection, and they repay long study. Through them all runs his humor, his tolerance, his friendliness. He seemed to see people through rosy spectacles and to expect them all to like him as much as he liked them. A hint of his physical condition comes in one letter from Italy, written evidently in answer to a warning from William Clough. "Consumption be damned!" it begins. "It is consumption of cigarettes and chianti that interests me."

From *The Three Jovial Huntsmen*

While he was there he made the sketches for a book of Mrs. Comyns Carr called *North Italian Folk; Sketches of Town and Country Life*. It was published by Chatto and Windus in 1878. Later it was re-issued by Scribner and Welford in New York in a limited, numbered edition with the drawings colored by hand. It is a fortunate person who now owns one of the two hundred and fifty copies. Few artists have caught as well the background and atmosphere of the northern Mediterranean coast and the High Apennines. The full-page drawing of the flower girl in Genoa sitting, with her flowers around her, in an old gateway that leads into the Royal Palace is one of the loveliest of his designs. Full of humor is the sketch of a carnival figure standing in a little cart drawn by a mild and patient donkey. Everyone who has been in Italy will recognize with delight the little servant girl ready for her First Communion, with the white veil drawn back from the delicate, dark-eyed face. His drawings of the High Apennines give an authentic and vivid impression of those tiny gardens and vineyards carved out of the great flanks of the mountains that the Italians call "piani." The great chestnut trees that mean so much to the Apennine peasants are there, and the little stone bridges, with their graceful, sturdy lines, that span the swift mountain streams. Mrs. Carr's text is informing but a bit didactic. Caldecott's sketches are priceless.

In 1879 he took a small house in the country near Seven Oaks. There is a sketch of it in the volume of his sketches edited by Henry Blackburn. Underneath it Caldecott wrote, "My country house—Wybournes." The years that followed were probably the happiest of his life and were certainly the most productive· He was working on the picture books with his models all around him. One can imagine him getting up on the frosty autumn mornings to watch the hounds streaming by, followed by the red-coated huntsmen; chatting in the marketplace with the farmers; standing in the farmyards to sketch the pigs and hens; sitting on a hillside in summer to draw those fine, strong lines that define forever the fields and roads and hills of the English countryside. "I am now living," he wrote a friend in London, "in this quiet, out-of-the-way village in order to make some studies of animals—to wit horses, dogs and other human beings—which I wish to use for the work I shall be busy with during the coming winter." Some of the letters from Seven Oaks show how high his spirits were. In one to William Clough he draws a line around the conventional heading of his writing paper making it the signpost of an Inn. Then he sketches a horseman galloping madly by toward a distant village. Under it he writes: "Remember me to all friends who ask after or take an interest in me—whether bankers, accountants, fiddlers, farm agents, lawyers, artists, teetotallers or gentlemen." This was in 1880. In the same year he wrote a letter that rather discourages any hint of a romance with Kate Greenaway, although we know that she greatly admired his work. "I told Kate Greenaway something of what you said *re* her book," the letter runs. "Here is a note from her for you to look at. Perhaps you will send it back. She is, as you ask me, nearly thirty—maybe more—and not beautiful."

In the spring of 1880 he wrote a letter, filled with obvious pride and happiness, announcing his engagement to Marion H. Brind. They were married in the same year. He does not say very much about his wife in subsequent letters, but the "I" of the earlier correspondence becomes "we." Evidently she went everywhere with him. A fitting celebration of his marriage was the publication soon after the wedding day of *The Three Jovial Huntsmen*.

It was in 1879 that he first met Juliana Horatia Ewing. In describing their meeting, Miss Gatty, Mrs. Ewing's sister and biographer, says, "My sister was in London in June, 1879, and there made the acquaintance of Mr. Randolph Caldecott for whose illustrations to Washington Irving's *Old Christmas* and *Bracebridge Hall* she had an unbounded admiration, as well as for his toy books. This introduction led us to ask him, when *Jackanapes* was still simmering in Julie's brain, if he would supply a colored illustration for it. But as the tale was only written a very short time before it appeared, and because the illustration was wanted early because colors take long to print, Julie could not send the story to be read, but asked Mr.

Lob Lie-by-the-Fire

or the Luck of Lingborough

By Juliana Horatia Ewing

With Illustrations By Randolph Caldecott

Caldecott to draw her a picture to fit one of the scenes. The one she suggested was 'a fair-haired boy on a red-haired pony,' having noticed the artistic effect produced by this combination in one of her own nephews, a skillful seven-year-old rider who was accustomed to follow the hounds. This colored illustration was given to *Aunt Judy's Magazine* with the tale, but when it was re-published as a book in 1883 the scene was reproduced on a smaller scale in black and white only." Then Miss Gatty goes on to describe the career of *Jackanapes* in words that will find an echo in the hearts of illustrators today: "The first copies were brought out in dull stone-colored paper covers, and that powerful vehicle the Trade, unable to believe that a jewel could be concealed in so plain a casket, refused the work of J.H.E. and R.C. until they had stretched the paper cover on boards and colored the Union Jack which adorns it! No doubt the Trade understands its fickle child, the Public, better than either authors or artists do, and knows by experience that it requires tempting with what is pretty to look at before it tastes." Beside the illustrations for *Jackanapes, Lob Lie-by-the-Fire* and *Daddy Darwin's Dovecote,* Caldecott designed a new cover for *Aunt Judy's Magazine* and a cover for Miss Gatty's biography of her sister published after Mrs. Ewing's death. The drawing shows a sad little girl laying a wreath of flowers on a grave marked "J.H.E. May, 1885."

Caldecott and Mrs. Ewing had a good deal in common in their feeling for birds. Of her, Miss Gatty writes: "Julie did not touch much on bird pets in any of her tales, chiefly because she never kept one, having too much sympathy with their powers and their craving for flight to reconcile herself to keeping them in cages. . . . Major Ewing remembers how often she used to wish, when passing bird shops, that she could 'buy the whole collection and set them all free'—a desire which suggests a quaint version of her in Seven Dials with a mixed flock of macaws, canaries, parrots and thrushes shrieking and flying around her head!"

The Artist

Caldecott's feeling for birds must have made his drawings for *Daddy Darwin's Dovecote* a labor of love. His pocket notebooks are filled with the details of birds, some of them with penciled notes beside them indicating changes that he would make in the finished drawing—little directions like "longer beak" or "front hock like this" or "inside hock." Perhaps some of these detailed studies were used when he made his oil paintings of storks and pelicans for decorative screens. In 1881 George Routledge published Mrs. Frederick Locker's little book *What the Blackbird Said*. It was illustrated by Caldecott with four drawings in black and white, showing three birds, a robin, a blackbird and a rook—or crow.

Another proof of his skill in making birds express all sorts of emotions is in the illustrations for a book called *The Owls of Olynn Belfry*. We do not know just who the author, A.Y.D., is but we feel fairly certain that she was a lady. Frederick Locker's bookplate is in the copy in the Parker Collection. Caldecott's characterization of the owls is individual and amusing and some of the other drawings are lovely in design. There is one of the homesick governess, Mlle. Marie, sitting under a tree pining for her native France. In the setting of an English garden she looks very French— and very attractive. There is a scene showing a churchyard with figures of the village people in the foreground and the church and belfry in the background. Best of all is a drawing, that would delight the children, of the old owl solemnly leading a tiny and exquisite fairy queen in a quadrille. The old gentleman is in formal evening clothes and is a bit conscious of his feet. He is pointing them neatly, but they are an owl's claws just as his head is an owl's head, with its wise eyes and rather prissy mouth.

We do not know just when Caldecott made the drawings for Hallam Tennyson's rhymed version of *Jack and the Beanstalk*. It was published by Macmillan in the year of his death—1886. Some of the drawings are in pencil, unfinished, but so well engraved that they are as clear as crystal.

An ELEGY on the DEATH of a MAD DOG.

WRITTEN
By
Dr GOLDSMITH

PICTURED
By
R. CALDECOTT

SUNG
By Master
BILL PRIMROSE

IN MEMORY OF TOBY

His treatment of the contrast in size between Jack and the giant and his wife is fascinating. The giant's house, his possessions and his wife are all in scale. Jack is always a tiny, defiant figure in the foreground. There is mischief and courage in every line of him. How children today would love these drawings! The giant is huge and clumsy and rather stupid, but his wife is a jolly, roly-poly person. The only thing about her that is frightening is that she is unusually *large*. The castle, as Jack sees it from the top of the beanstalk, is a thing of dreams—piled towers and turrets against the sky. The quality of humor in this book reminds us a little of Frank R. Stockton and his illustrator—E. B. Bensell. While Jack stands at the door of the giant's kitchen, watching the giant's wife and unseen by her, she is carefully basting a young elephant which she is evidently preparing for her husband's dinner. Neatly trussed and stuffed it lies in the huge pan on its side, looking very brown and tempting. In the drawing where Jack has

From *The Fox Jumped Over the Parson's Gate*

the hen under his arm and is rushing for the beanstalk, he is running so fast that you can feel the push of the wind against him. This tale has been a favorite with the children for centuries. It would be very exciting if the children of today could have Caldecott's interpretation of it.

While he was making these illustrations and working away at his painting and modeling, the picture books were parading gaily in to and out of the presses. Boys and girls were claiming them, and they were winning praise from even the most carping critics of art and literature. The single copies sold for the sum of one shilling. So did Mrs. Ewing's books, which were published by The Society for Promoting Christian Knowledge. We pay a higher price for them now, but how well they are worth it! How many members of an older generation in America today think of the English countryside in terms of Caldecott's fields and farmyards and village streets? When we see England for the first time it is familiar to many of us because we knew as children the Caldecott picture books. France published only one of them—a volume of the sketches that had appeared in English magazines called *Nouvelles Scènes Humoristiques*. It is in color and was brought to Paris by Hachette & Cie. in a de luxe edition in 1887. There is a copy in the Parker Collection.

Early in 1886 Caldecott went with his wife to the United States, planning to sketch our American background and the people. They went to Florida, again seeking a warmer climate and the sun, and he died at St. Augustine on February 12th—Lincoln's Birthday. Modern medical science probably could have saved him. Not nearly as much was known then of the disease that was sapping his strength and vitality. His letters show that he himself had an unfailing optimism and courage—an important asset in fighting tuberculosis. It is tragic that he could not have lived to picture the American scene. His tolerance and gaiety, his genius for background and characterization might have made a record of great and lasting value.

From *The Farmer's Boy*

Two years after his death his friends and fellow artists arranged an exhibit of his work at the Brasenose Club in Manchester. Many of the exhibits were lent by Mrs. Caldecott. She sent, too, his last photograph with a little note, saying, "His friends think that he looks sad and ill, but I feel that this is more like him than any of the others." Studying it, we feel that she must have been right. The clear, calm eyes and wide brow have the light directly on them. The humor evident in some of the early photographs and in the sketches is missing, but in its place there is strength and purpose. This photograph is used as the frontispiece for the catalogue: *Catalogue of a Loan Collection of the Works of Randolph Caldecott. Exhibited by The Brasenose Club. Manchester, 1888.* The tributes that were paid him by the great and near-great of his day are recorded.

41

Beside his published drawings Caldecott made drawings for two alphabets. They are both in color, four and three-quarter inches by four and five-eighths. The "sporting" alphabet is in rich browns and greens and yellows, illustrating scenes of hunting, fishing, rowing, swimming, etc. The other one is very much like the picture books. In it his humor and his imagination are given full play. In the drawing that represents the letter U a man is walking along a village street in the rain carrying a very impressive umbrella. At his feet stands a tiny green frog who is apparently just getting ready to walk along beside him. He carries a large green lily pad! Both these alphabets are now in the Parker Collection.

No matter where one lives, it is worth while to make a pilgrimage to Cambridge to see this Collection. Here in the Houghton Library at Harvard is one of his oil paintings, several of the bas-reliefs, many original drawings, first and special editions of the books, and—most revealing of all—the notebooks and letters. It is worth while to go there just to see the special edition of *The Queen of Hearts*. The color in it—the warm reds and browns, the delicate blues and greens—set in our mind forever the color that he meant them all to have. The notebooks take you with him through the early years, through his travels on the Continent and into the richest and most productive period—1876 to the year of his death. His personal letters, often to men and women who were distinguished figures in the world of art and literature, give a vivid sense not only of the man himself but of his time. First of all he reflects England and English life, but the letters and sketches from Germany and France and Italy show a shrewd observation, an appreciation of character as well as of the scene, that gives them great value. They, much more than the picture books, tell of a world that is gone but it is a world that some of us like to remember. It is easy to see in both his letters and his sketches that *people* fascinated Caldecott—all sorts and kinds of people. If he saw them as slightly ridiculous, pompous, conceited or self-conscious he drew them that way. But

From *The Three Jovial Huntsmen*

there is no malice in his interpretation. They were figures in a scene that told a story—funny, sad, romantic, commonplace. Not even the smallest detail is left out of the story. It is all there for us to read.

His art stands, too, for the unchanging things—for the precious possessions that are common to all men; for the fields and hills and streams, for the flight of birds and the companionship of friendly animals, for the beauty of bare trees in winter and the delicate color and outline of their branches in spring. There was no fixed idea in his mind, apparently, of making an "arrangement" of his background and his models. There is always design, but it is Nature's design rather than his own. He saw things as they are. Even when he gives Miss Mousie a white muslin dress she remains a mouse; just as Mr. Frog in his green coat and flowered waistcoat remains unmistakably a frog. And through it all runs his humor, the gaiety that is to the children his most endearing quality. The laughter that is their tribute to him is quiet laughter; not loud guffaws, but a smile, that dawns in their eyes and touches their lips, or a low chuckle. He never puzzles them with broad caricature. To them he is always reasonable. Through his fertile imagination and his artist's skill they find the story—and are content.

Fifty-two years after Caldecott's death in St. Augustine, Frederic Melcher established the Caldecott Medal. It was awarded first, in 1938, to Dorothy Lathrop's *Animals of the Bible*. A committee of librarians selects each year the most distinguished picture book by an American artist published during the preceding year and the Medal is presented at the annual meeting of The American Library Association. The award serves a double purpose. It honors the young artists who are entering the field of children's books. And it helps to keep the memory of Randolph Caldecott green. A fellow artist who knew him well said, after his death, that his name would "remain till the end of our art and literature a household word." He was speaking, probably, only of England. For his birthday party in 1946 we might blow out the hundred candles with one long, steady breath and wish that his name might be "a household word" to all the children of all the world.

Bibliography

THE PICTURE BOOKS

THE DIVERTING HISTORY OF JOHN GILPIN. Engraved by Edmund Evans. London. George Routledge & Sons. 1878. Later; London and New York. Frederick Warne & Company.

THE HOUSE THAT JACK BUILT. The Same. 1878.

THE BABES IN THE WOODS. The Same. 1879.

ELEGY ON THE DEATH OF A MAD DOG. By Oliver Goldsmith. The Same. 1879.

THE THREE JOVIAL HUNTSMEN. The Same. 1880.

SING A SONG FOR SIXPENCE. The Same. 1880.

THE QUEEN OF HEARTS. The Same. 1881.

THE FARMER'S BOY. The Same. 1881.

THE MILKMAID. The Same. 1882.

HEY DIDDLE DIDDLE. The Same. 1882.

A FROG HE WOULD A-WOOING GO. The Same. 1883.

THE FOX JUMPED OVER THE PARSON'S GATE. The Same. 1883.

COME LASSIES AND LADS. The Same. 1884.

RIDE A COCK HORSE TO BANBURY CROSS. The Same. 1884.

A FARMER WENT TROTTING UPON HIS GRAY MARE. The Same. 1884.

MRS. MARY BLAIZE. By Oliver Goldsmith. The Same. 1885.

THE GREAT PANJANDRUM HIMSELF. The Same. 1885.

Miniature Edition in Single Copies and in Four Volumes. London and New York. Frederick Warne & Company.

THE COMPLETE COLLECTION OF RANDOLPH CALDECOTT'S PICTURES AND SONGS. With a Preface by Austin Dobson. Edmund Evans, Engraver and Printer. London. George Routledge & Sons. 1887. Limited Edition.

45

THE HARZ MOUNTAINS; A TOUR IN THE TOY COUNTRY. By Henry Blackburn. Illustrated by Randolph Caldecott. London. Sampson Low, Marston & Company. 1872.

OLD CHRISTMAS; SELECTIONS FROM THE SKETCH BOOK BY WASHINGTON IRVING. With Illustrations by Randolph Caldecott. London. The Macmillan Company. 1876.

BRACEBRIDGE HALL; SELECTIONS FROM THE SKETCH BOOK BY WASHINGTON IRVING. With Illustrations by Randolph Caldecott. London. The Macmillan Company. 1877.

NORTH ITALIAN FOLK; SKETCHES OF TOWN AND COUNTRY LIFE. By Mrs. Comyns Carr. With Sketches by Randolph Caldecott. London. Chatto and Windus. 1878. Later; New York. Scribner & Welford. Limited Edition.

BRETON FOLK; AN ARTISTIC TOUR IN BRITTANY. By Henry Blackburn. With Sketches by Randolph Caldecott. London. Sampson Low, Marston & Company. 1880.

WHAT THE BLACKBIRD SAID. By Mrs. Frederick Locker. Illustrated by Randolph Caldecott. London. George Routledge & Sons. 1881.

A SKETCH-BOOK OF R. CALDECOTT'S; ORIGINAL SKETCHES FOR THE FOUR SEASONS. Reproduced by Edmund Evans, the Engraver and Printer. London. George Routledge & Sons. 1883.

SOME OF AESOP'S FABLES WITH MODERN INSTANCES. Shown in Designs by Randolph Caldecott. From New Translations by Alfred Caldecott. Engravings by James Cooper. London. The Macmillan Company. 1883.

JACKANAPES. By Juliana Horatia Ewing. With a Frontispiece by Randolph Caldecott. London. The Society for Promoting Christian Knowledge. 1883.

DADDY DARWIN'S DOVECOTE. By Juliana Horatia Ewing. Illustrated by Randolph Caldecott. London. The Society for Promoting Christian Knowledge. 1884.

THE OWLS OF OLYNN BELFRY. By A.Y.D. Illustrated by Randolph Caldecott. London. Chatto & Windus.

JACK AND THE BEANSTALK. By Hallam Tennyson. With Illustrations by Randolph Caldecott. London. The Macmillan Company. 1886.

Lᴏʙ Lɪᴇ-ʙʏ-ᴛʜᴇ-Fɪʀᴇ. By Juliana Horatia Ewing. With Illustrations by
Randolph Caldecott. London. The Society for Promoting Christian
Knowledge.

Rᴀɴᴅᴏʟᴘʜ Cᴀʟᴅᴇᴄᴏᴛᴛ's Sᴋᴇᴛᴄʜᴇs. With an Introduction by Henry
Blackburn. London. Sampson Low, Marston & Company. Second Edition. 1889.

From *A Frog He Would A-Wooing Go*